Henderson

by Iain Gray

Lang**Syne**
PUBLISHING
WRITING *to* REMEMBER

Lang**Syne**

PUBLISHING

WRITING *to* REMEMBER

79 Main Street, Newtongrange,
Midlothian EH22 4NA
Tel: 0131 344 0414   Fax: 0845 075 6085
E-mail: info@lang-syne.co.uk
www.langsyneshop.co.uk

Design by Dorothy Meikle
Printed by Printwell Ltd
© Lang Syne Publishers Ltd 2017

ISBN 978-1-85217-107-0

Henderson

SEPT AND RELATED NAMES:

Eanrig
Enderson
Enrick
Henders
Hendersone
Hendersoun
Hendrie
Hendry
Hennerson
Hennryson
Henrici
Kendrick
Kenrick
MacEnrick
MacHendrick
MacHendrie
MacHendry

SOLA VIRTUS NOBILITAT

Henderson

MOTTO:
Virtue alone ennobles.

CREST:
A hand holding a six-pointed star,
surrounded by a crescent.

TERRITORY:
Dumfriesshire, Borders, Fife,
Glencoe, Caithness, Shetland Islands.

Chapter one:

The origins of the clan system

by Rennie McOwan

The original Scottish clans of the Highlands and the great families of the Lowlands and Borders were gatherings of families, relatives, allies and neighbours for mutual protection against rivals or invaders.

Scotland experienced invasion from the Vikings, the Romans and English armies from the south. The Norman invasion of what is now England also had an influence on land-holding in Scotland. Some of these invaders stayed on and in time became 'Scottish'.

The word clan derives from the Gaelic language term 'clann', meaning children, and it was first used many centuries ago as communities were formed around tribal lands in glens and mountain fastnesses.

The format of clans changed over the centuries, but at its best the chief and his family held the land on behalf of all, like trustees, and the ordinary clansmen and women believed they had a blood relationship with the founder of their clan.

There were two way duties and obligations. An inadequate chief could be deposed and replaced by someone of greater ability.

Clan people had an immense pride in race. Their relationship with the chief was like adult children to a father and they had a real dignity.

The concept of clanship is very old and a more feudal notion of authority gradually crept in.

Pictland, for instance, was divided into seven principalities ruled by feudal leaders who were the strongest and most charismatic leaders of their particular groups.

By the sixth century the 'British' kingdoms of Strathclyde, Lothian and Celtic Dalriada (Argyll) had emerged and Scotland, as one nation, began to take shape in the time of King Kenneth MacAlpin.

Some chiefs claimed descent from

ancient kings which may not have been accurate in every case.

By the twelfth and thirteenth centuries the clans and families were more strongly brought under the central control of Scottish monarchs.

Lands were awarded and administered more and more under royal favour, yet the power of the area clan chiefs was still very great.

The long wars to ensure Scotland's independence against the expansionist ideas of English monarchs extended the influence of some clans and reduced the lands of others.

Those who supported Scotland's greatest king, Robert the Bruce, were awarded the territories of the families who had opposed his claim to the Scottish throne.

In the Scottish Borders country – the notorious Debatable Lands – the great families built up a ferocious reputation for providing warlike men accustomed to raiding into England and occasionally fighting one another.

Chiefs had the power to dispense justice and to confiscate lands and clan warfare produced a society where martial virtues – courage, hardiness, tenacity – were greatly admired.

Gradually the relationship between the clans and the Crown became strained as Scottish monarchs became more orientated to life in the Lowlands and, on occasion, towards England.

The Highland clans spoke a different language, Gaelic, whereas the language of Lowland Scotland and the court was Scots and in more modern times, English.

Highlanders dressed differently, had different customs, and their wild mountain land sometimes seemed almost foreign to people living in the Lowlands.

It must be emphasised that Gaelic culture was very rich and story-telling, poetry, piping, the clarsach (harp) and other music all flourished and were greatly respected.

Highland culture was different from other parts of Scotland but it was not inferior or less sophisticated.

Central Government, whether in London or Edinburgh, sometimes saw the Gaelic clans as

"The spirit of the clan means much to thousands of people"

a challenge to their authority and some sent expeditions into the Highlands and west to crush the power of the Lords of the Isles.

Nevertheless, when the eighteenth century Jacobite Risings came along the cause of the Stuarts was mainly supported by Highland clans.

The word Jacobite comes from the Latin for James – Jacobus. The Jacobites wanted to restore the exiled Stuarts to the throne of Britain.

The monarchies of Scotland and England became one in 1603 when King James VI of Scotland (1st of England) gained the English throne after Queen Elizabeth died.

The Union of Parliaments of Scotland and England, the Treaty of Union, took place in 1707.

Some Highland clans, of course, and Lowland families opposed the Jacobites and supported the incoming Hanoverians.

After the Jacobite cause finally went down at Culloden in 1746 a kind of ethnic cleansing took place. The power of the chiefs was curtailed. Tartan and the pipes were banned in law.

Many emigrated, some because they

wanted to, some because they were evicted by force. In addition, many Highlanders left for the cities of the south to seek work.

Many of the clan lands became home to sheep and deer shooting estates.

But the warlike traditions of the clans and the great Lowland and Border families lived on, with their descendants fighting bravely for freedom in two world wars.

Remember the men from whence you came, says the Gaelic proverb, and to that could be added the role of many heroic women.

The spirit of the clan, of having roots, whether Highland or Lowland, means much to thousands of people.

Chapter two:

Lowlanders and Highlanders

From the extreme south to the extreme north of Scotland, Hendersons have flourished for centuries and been at the forefront of important events in Scotland's long history.

In many cases, however, while the numerous Hendersons throughout the world share the same surname, they do not share a common heritage. This is because 'Henderson', quite simply, means 'son of Hendry', and there were many such 'sons' of numerous 'Hendrys' to be found not only in Scotland itself but also throughout Europe.

The original form of the name in Scotland was 'Henryson', later adapted to Henderson.

The surnames of MacHendrie, MacHendry, Hendry, and Hendrie, although similar to Henderson, have no official relationship, and are regarded as septs of the MacNaughton clan.

Lowland families of Henderson origin are known to have been settled in Dumfriesshire at least as early as the twelfth century, while in 1374 a William Henderson is recorded as holding the powerful post of chamberlain of Lochmaben Castle, reputed to have been the birthplace 100 years earlier of Robert the Bruce.

The Hendersons spread eastwards from Dumfriesshire into the Border lands of Liddesdale, where they became one of the famed riding clans.

Unlike other Border clans such as the Douglases, Kerrs, Elliots, Armstrongs, and Maxwells, however, the Hendersons appear not to have taken any significant part in the bitter and bloody feuds that made much of the lawless Borders a virtual no-go area for outsiders.

This is borne out by the fact that the Hendersons are conspicuous by their absence from a list of Border clans who were subjected to dire 'letters of fire and sword' during the reign of James VI as punishment for their unruly behaviour.

A number of the original Dumfriesshire-Borders Hendersons moved to Ireland during what was known as the Plantation of Ulster from 1609 to 1613, and many of them are believed to have subsequently immigrated to North America.

A descendant of Dumfriesshire- Borders Hendersons, James Henderson was appointed Lord Advocate for Scotland under James IV at some time around 1494.

The family's power and influence received a huge boost in 1511 when he acquired the rich lands and baronetcy of Fordell, near Dalgety Bay, Fife.

It was from this date that 'Henderson of Fordell' became the designation of the chiefs of the Hendersons of the Lowlands, and in 1985 the Lord Lyon King of Arms of Scotland recognised Dr. John William Henderson of Fordell as chief of the baronial house of Fordell and chief of the name and arms of Henderson.

Dr. Henderson's great-grandfather had emigrated from Scotland to Australia in 1839, and on Dr. Henderson's death in 2004 his son, Alistair, who lives in Brisbane, Australia, succeeded to his titles.

Built originally as a fortified mansion, Fordell is no longer in the hands of the Henderson family, and at one time was renowned as the home of the colourful and controversial former Solicitor General for Scotland, Nicholas Fairbairn, QC.

Unrelated to the Hendersons of Fordell are completely separate families of Henderson whose territory was in Caithness and the Shetlands. The Hendersons of Caithness took their name from Hendry Gunn, a younger son of a 15th century chief of the Clan Gunn.

He split himself from his family as a means of avoiding the murderous feuds between his clan and the Keiths. The family he founded took their name from him, as 'sons of Hendry', or Hendersons.

The Hendersons of the Shetland Islands

trace their descent from a William Magnusson who ruled part of the sprawling territory in the name of a Norse king who also held sovereignty over Sweden, Denmark, and Orkney.

His son, Henry Williamson, gave the name Henryson, or Henderson, to succeeding generations.

Another family of Henderson are those Hendersons who once held the wild and rugged lands that embraced Glencoe, both sides of Loch Leven, and Ardnamurchan.

Eanruig Mor MacRigh Neachtan is the Gaelic form of 'Big Hendry', a son of the Pictish king Nectan, who ruled in the early years of the eighth century.

From this 'Big Hendry' descended the MacEanruig ('sons of Hendry') chiefs who at an undetermined date held the Glencoe lands until Robert the Bruce, victor of Bannockburn in 1314, granted the lordship to the MacDonald Lords of the Isles as reward for their valiant military service.

Holding their lands under the vassalage

of the Lords of the Isles, the Hendersons became known as the MacIains of Glencoe.

This was after a daughter of Dugald MacEanruig, the last Henderson of Glencoe clan chief, married a MacDonald, and their son was subsequently granted Glencoe.

This son, known variously as Iain Fraoch, MacIain of Glencoe, and Iain Abrach, appointed the Hendersons as both his hereditary pipers and bodyguard at some stage in the 1340s.

They were also accorded the ancient Celtic honour of being the first to 'lift', or raise, a chief's body when it was being carried for burial.

Chapter three:

Massacre and conspiracy

It was in their role of bodyguards to the MacDonald chiefs of Glencoe that the Hendersons were involved in one of the bloodiest episodes in Scotland's grim history.

This was the Massacre of Glencoe, of February 13, 1692, when a Henderson died while bravely attempting to defend the life of his chief.

Although a Jacobite rebellion had been quashed in 1689, one year after James VII had fled to exile in France and William of Orange had been invited to take the united thrones of England and Scotland, the Highlands were still in a ferment of unrest.

This required the garrisoning of troops throughout the Highlands – troops that were badly needed to fight in the foreign wars in which William was engaged.

The problem was how to quell the unrest and pacify the clans that still adhered to the forlorn Jacobite cause.

A meeting of clan chiefs was convened near Bridge of Orchy, in Perthshire, in June of 1691, and all clans that had fought against the government were granted an amnesty on condition that their chiefs signed a personal oath of allegiance to William, before a magistrate, no later than January 1, 1692.

The Secretary of State for Scotland, Sir John Dalrymple, the Master of Stair, was convinced that not all of the clan chiefs would sign the required oath, and accordingly laid plans to punish those who refused.

As a result of circumstances that were beyond his control, Alasdair MacIain, the 12th clan chief of the Glencoe MacDonalds, was late in meeting the required deadline and his name was ominously not entered on the all-important list of those who had signed. The Master of Stair saw his opportunity and resolved to make a harsh example of the MacDonalds of Glencoe.

A secret commission to carry this out was given to Captain Robert Campbell of Glenlyon, who took a force of about 140 men from Argyll's regiment to Glencoe, armed with a warrant to quarter his men in the homes of the MacDonalds who lived at the bottom of the glen.

Glenlyon and his soldiers spent nearly two weeks enjoying the hospitality of the 500 or so MacDonalds among whom they had been quartered. This was a hospitality destined to be infamously and murderously abused.

Orders finally arrived for Glenlyon to fall upon the unsuspecting MacDonalds and massacre them – sparing no one under the age of 70, women and children not excepted.

The exact figure is not known, but in the early hours of February 13, 1692, at least 38 men, women, and children were slaughtered while countless others died in the severe snowstorm into which they had fled.

MacIain of Glencoe was cold-bloodedly shot as he attempted to rise from his bed, despite the valiant attempt of his bodyguard and

personal piper, known as Henderson of the
Chanters, to save his life.

Described as a man of great height and
strength, Henderson was brutally cut down by the
sabre-wielding soldiers.

Hendersons were also involved in two
other bloody incidents in 17th century Scotland.

One was the mysterious affair known as
the Gowrie Conspiracy, of August 5, 1600, the
truth behind which has never been satisfactorily
determined even up to the present day.

James VI had apparently been about to set
off on his favourite pastime of hunting when he
was approached by Alexander, the young Master
of Ruthven, and brother of the Earl of Gowrie.

He had a strange tale to relate. He
claimed he had discovered a man attempting to
bury a cache of gold coins in a field outside Perth,
and urged the king to come with him to meet the
man and see the gold.

The avaricious James complied, and
when he came to Gowrie House, in Perth, he was
ushered into a turret room by the young Master.

The 'official' account of what subsequently transpired after the unsuspecting king entered the room is that its sole occupant was a man dressed in armour.

This 'man in armour' was one Alexander Henderson, the Earl of Gowrie's chamberlain.

The Master of Ruthven is said to have followed the king into the room and drawn a dagger, telling his monarch he was going to kill him in revenge for his role in the death of his father.

James managed to shout for help from the window of the turret and one of his courtiers rushed in and stabbed the Master to death. The Earl of Gowrie, following close on the heels of the courtier and others who had dashed to the king's aid, was also stabbed to death.

Alexander Henderson was closely questioned, and apparently claimed that he had been forced into a plot to kill the king. Bafflingly, however, he was not only promptly pardoned by James, but granted lands in Perthshire.

The truth of the mysterious affair is

impossible to untangle, but James certainly had a motive for arranging the deaths of both the Earl of Gowrie and his brother, because he owed the family the not inconsiderable sum of £80,000.

There are also dark hints that the complex Stuart monarch had homosexual leanings, and that the death of the young Master may have resulted from a botched attempt by James to seduce him.

Nearly 80 years later, in May of 1679, all of Scotland was stunned when the powerful Archbishop of St. Andrews, James Sharp, was unceremoniously dragged from his coach on Magus Muir, Fife, and hacked to death.

Hated by those Presbyterians known as the Covenanters for his attempts to enforce the Episcopalian form of worship on Scotland, Sharp had been en route from Edinburgh to his opulent residence at St. Andrews when his murderers struck.

They were led by John Balfour of Kinloch and his brother-in-law David Hackston of Rathillet, and among their number was one

John Henderson, believed to have been either a Fife farmer or a weaver.

Chapter four:

For country and Covenant

John Henderson had struck a militant blow for the Presbyterian faith through his part in the murder of Archbishop Sharp, but more than 40 years earlier another Henderson from Fife had made a more significant and enduring contribution.

This was the minister Alexander Henderson, a member of a cadet branch of the Hendersons of Fordell. Born in Fife around 1583, Alexander Henderson is renowned as one of the 'fathers' of the landmark National Covenant of 1638.

Educated at St. Andrews University, he had by about 1611 become a professor of philosophy, but later became a minister at Leuchars, in his native Fife.

An inspired preacher and staunch defender

of Presbyterian doctrine, Henderson was implacably opposed to the stubborn attempts by Charles I to impose a new order of religious services, known as the Book of Common Prayer, on Scotland.

Henderson was at the forefront of the protest movement that unsuccessfully petitioned Charles to revoke his order for the imposition of the prayer book.

One form the protest took occurred in July of 1637 when Jenny Geddes famously lobbed her stool at a minister in Edinburgh's St. Giles Kirk while he was attempting to read from the hated book.

Matters came to a head when Henderson and the Edinburgh lawyer Archibald Johnston of Wariston co-authored the National Covenant – a document as important to Scottish history as the famed Declaration of Arbroath of 1320.

Described as 'the glorious marriage day of the kingdom with God', the Covenant renounced Catholic belief, pledged to uphold the

Presbyterian religion, and called for free parliaments and assemblies.

Signed at Edinburgh's Greyfriars Church on February 28, 1638 by Scotland's nobles, barons, burgesses and ministers, it was subscribed to the following day by hundreds of ordinary people.

Copies were made and dispatched around Scotland and signed by thousands more.

In 1643, when the English parliament was embroiled in civil war with Charles I, Henderson drafted the Solemn League and Covenant, in which the Scots pledged armed support for the Parliamentarians in return for a guarantee to reform religion in England and to preserve Presbyterianism in Scotland.

In the constantly changing climate of the civil war, Charles I found himself in 1646 in the hands of the Scots army at Newcastle. It was here that the doomed monarch engaged in a celebrated debate with Alexander Henderson on religion and church government.

Henderson died shortly afterwards, on August 19, and monarchists claimed this was

God's punishment for his audacity in daring to argue with the divinely ordained Charles!

Fittingly, Alexander Henderson was buried in Greyfriars Churchyard where there is a monument to his memory.

The churchyard is also the final resting place of another noted Henderson – Thomas Henderson, who achieved fame as an astronomer.

Born in Dundee in 1798, he carried out important astronomical investigations that included cataloguing the positions of stars.

He was appointed the first Astronomer Royal for Scotland in 1834, and until his death ten years later recorded more than 60,000 celestial observations from the former observatory on Edinburgh's Calton Hill.

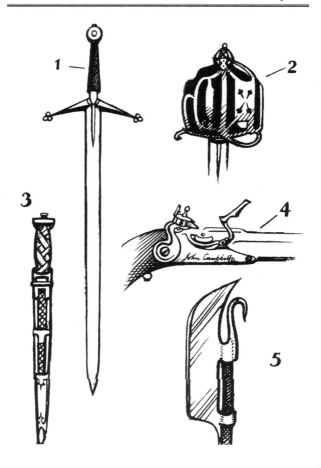

Clan weapons

1)   The claymore or two-handed sword
        (fifteenth or early sixteenth century)

2)   Basket hilt of broadsword
        made in Stirling, 1716

3)   Highland dirk
        (eighteenth century)

4)   Steel pistol *(detail)* made in Doune

5)   Head of Lochaber Axe as carried
        in the '45 and earlier